11/22
STRAND PRICE
$ 7.00

THE 100 BEST
BATHROOMS

BETA-PLUS

THE 100 BEST
BATHROOMS

CONTENTS

THE BATHROOM OF A CONTEMPORARY MAISON DE MAÎTRE

This town house in the heart of Antwerp dates from the end of the nineteenth century. The property had suffered over the years from the changing use and numerous renovations and modifications. Hans Verstuyft Architects restored the residence in a contemporary and respectful way: a renewing approach but yet not forming a break with the past. Materials and colours were used consistently that made the original architecture visible and emphasised it. Other additions (new floors, light fittings, etc.) were custom designed by the architect and seamlessly integrated into the authentic whole. The interior was planned soberly; new elements are based on what might once have been there. The bathroom is contemporary but with a classic touch.

www.hansverstuyftarchitecten.be

The bathroom is given a classic touch with the use of Carrara marble and dark wood. The link to the past can also be felt here.

AN OPEN PLAN BATHROOM

The interior architecture agency Minus was given the task to create the design of an L-shaped loft, a conversion from an old cotton mill with annexed new built wing. All the functions were linked to these two right-angled wings.

www.minus.be

The open plan bathroom consists of a bathroom and hand basin volume, both finished in Corian. The grey glass partition visually shields the toilet.

A SOBER ATMOSPHERE

The Brion Leclercq (Julie Brion & Tanguy Leclercq A.D.) agency realised
the interior layout of an urban penthouse located in Brussels. Always with the desire to make the
ambiance uniform and smooth, the architectural idea for the bathrooms consisted of choosing
a limited range of materials and, in particular, using a simple material in multiple forms.

www.brionleclercq.com

A large art deco polished steel mirror designed by the interior architects conceals the various storage areas in the bathroom.

A REAL METAMORPHOSIS

A rustic villa with a lot of oak and dark materials was transformed by Peter Ivens (interior and architecture agency Astra Loves Living) into a modern country residence: the residence experienced a true metamorphosis through a few strong interventions.

www.astralovesliving.com

The old attic on the top floor was furnished as a master bedroom with dressing room and bathroom.
Shower with coarse mosaics combined with natural stone in Sahara beige (Troubleyn).

THE BATHROOM OF A COSY WEEKEND HOME

Interior architect Marie-France Stadsbader transformed two semi-detached houses on the coast into a cosy weekend home for a young family. Despite the limited surface each function was still given its space.

mst@cantillana.com

The bathrooms exude rest because Marie-France chose understated materials.

TEAK WOOD AND CARRARA MARBLE

This seaside apartment was given a thorough facelift by interior architect Marie-France Stadsbader and was then carried out by Obumex. The circulation was revised completely, all the small spaces and numerous doors were reduced to the strictly necessary. Perspectives were created from each place to give as much sense of space as possible and also to draw in the light. The natural materials teak and Carrara marble can be found throughout the apartment but always used in a different way so that everything is in harmony.

mst@cantillana.com

The bathroom was created completely in worked Carrara marble, made with a glass mosaic by the company Van den Weghe.

LIGHT AND TRANSPARENCY IN A HISTORIC FARMHOUSE

A historic farmhouse has been transformed by Virginie & Odile Dejaegere
(Dejaegere Interiors) into a contemporary living space.
All axes in the house, including the *en suite* bedroom, bathroom
and dressing room, have direct access to the garden.

dejaegere_interiors@hotmail.com

The master bathroom has been finished with tadelakt. The floor is clad with white pebble stones. The bathtub is covered with oak planks.

The wall between the shower entrance and the hammam is clad with old oak planks.

A HEAVENLY PLEASURE

Waterl'Eau offers intense moments of relaxation and wellness for the bathroom. For more than fifteen years now, they are the specialist for exclusive bathroom equipment. In their "private" showroom in Antwerp, one can see and touch the fine materials that make bathing a heavenly pleasure. Taps and accessories by Volevatch of Paris, Czech & Speake, Lefroy Brooks, Samuel Heath. Fine basins from Italy, France and England. And bath cosmetics from Waterl'Eau.

www.waterleau-shop.be

This bathroom is a design by interior architect Marianne Swyzen.
She selected Volevatch taps from the Bistrot range, which harmonise perfectly with the white Carrara marble and the wooden floor.

PROGRESSIVE KNOW-HOW,
PASSIONATE AUTHENTICITY

Whenever living is experienced as "coming home", the desire grows to have each room tastefully come into its own. Frank Tack has again allowed his know-how to speak, to tastefully design the interior of this manor house, designed by the architect Bernard De Clerck, into a harmonious whole.

www.franktack.eu

The sober, rustic style is translated in an enthusiastic way in this philosophy of living. Each lovingly created piece of furniture by Frank Tack according to the traditional craft exudes this atmosphere. The customised handmade craft, integrated in a refined way in the whole, offers a top quality look in this exceptional realisation. The exclusive, durable wood exudes class and comfort. The harmonious interplay of noble materials predominates: a passion for perfection and top quality craftsmanship.

HANDMADE CRAFTSMANSHIP
AS A GUIDING PRINCIPLE

In this report on the stone company Van den Weghe – The Stonecompany a few recent projects are shown with handmade craftsmanship as a guiding principle: perfection in custom-made stone as a result of over thirty years' experience in the top segment.

www.vandenweghe.be

This bathroom combines Belgian Rouge Griotte stone (wall cladding) with Bianco Statuario (as the work surface, on the floor and skirting) in this bathroom.

Master bathroom clad
in very large panels of
Emperador Dark.
The floor is covered with
Crema Marfil.

Traditional craftsmanship from the natural stone company Van den Weghe installed by Themenos in an English manor: Fior di Bosco natural stone with a lot of moulding work combined with a parquet floor.

This blend of custom-made Fior di Bosco and the warmth of natural oak creates a very intimate and classic atmosphere.

THE ECLECTIC RESTORATION
OF AN 18TH-CENTURY BASTIDE NEAR AIX

In the immediate surroundings of Aix-en-Provence, you can still find a number of well-preserved, majestic bastides dating from the seventeenth and eighteenth centuries. One of these bastides, idyllically situated in a conifer wood, has very recently been completely restored by the current owners. They chose to restore the eighteenth-century bastide to its former glory, while adding contemporary touches. This report features an eclectic and harmonious home: contemporary top design in combination with a historic site. The owners consulted Josselin Fleury from Designer's Studio in Aix-en-Provence: a design boutique and also a studio for interior design.

www.designers-studio.com

The bathroom of the lady of the house, with a Boffi bath in the centre.

BESIDE THE BAY OF SAINT-TROPEZ

This bathroom in a beautifully situated holiday home beside the bay of Saint-Tropez renovated by the Belgian architect Michel Lesot has been designed by Gilles de Meulemeester (Ebony Interiors).

www.ebony-interiors.com

The bathroom is clad with Antalya cream natural stone. Wall lamps by Liaigre, taps by Dornbracht.

A RETURN TO THE ESSENCE

This report illustrates the vision of Olivier Lempereur: removing
everything that is superficial and pointless, in order to find the essence
of a room. In this new building with a view of the Seine he has
created a light, functional triplex for a young married couple of architecture lovers:
a home that is a peaceful refuge. The bathroom exudes timeless elegance.

www.olivierlempereur.com

A harmony of natural stone and oak in this bathroom.

AN AUTHENTIC RESTORATION IN MONOCHROME WHITE

This distinctive residence from around the turn of the last century (ca. 1900)
has been subtly restored by architect Vincent Van Duysen for a family with young children.
Structurally, very little has been changed. With just a few minimal alterations, the
architect has succeeded in giving a contemporary touch to the new design:
together with the use of monochrome shades of white throughout, this has
created a living environment with an atmosphere of peace and serenity.

www.vincentvanduysen.com

A view of the main bathroom.   The guest lavatory.

A SENSE OF SPACE

This bathroom is clad with Unistone composite stone. Taps and shower fittings by Dornbracht. A sheet of glass has been installed by the bath, which, like the washbasins, is made of solid natural stone. The units are made of white-stained sandblasted oak. The mirror has a matt finish to allow a flatscreen to be incorporated. A design by Ensemble & Associés.

www.ensembleetassocies.be

CONTEMPORARY CLASSIC

The bathroom in the house of the antiques dealers Brigitte & Alain Garnier is as exceptional as their historic Vaucelleshof itself, an abbey and farmhouse complex including 17th, 18th and 19th century buildings acquired by the couple in 1999 and fully restored.

www.garnier.be

On the extreme right a 17th century Portuguese art cabinet in ivory and ebony.

The shower walls were covered in Carrara marble. The vaulted ceiling is finished in tadelakt.

↖
A Roman bath in Carrara marble (17th century). The floor, also in old Carrara marble, was supplied by Rik Storms.

A ZEN ATMOSPHERE

A house, built in the 1960s, was given a new look by AID Architects.
The right proportions ensure that the house has a
natural look and a calming atmosphere.

www.aidarchitecten.be

The interplay of light and materials creates an almost zen atmosphere in the bathroom.

HARMONY AND SPACE

A beautiful long-fronted farmhouse created by the great architect Raymond Rombouts was renovated by interior architect Alexis Herbosch. At the request of the owners, an extension was built and the interior of the farmhouse was completely renovated. The harmony of the proportions and the use of materials resulted in a complementary whole.

www.herbosch-vanreeth.be

The corridor past the oak wall units to the master bathroom.

A glass walk-in shower was selected to optimise the sense of space in the bathroom.

A BATHROOM CLAD WITH JURA STONE

Vlassak-Verhulst, the exclusive villa construction company, built this stately country house with a number of outbuildings. The house, situated in magnificent natural surroundings near the Dutch coast, was then handed over to Sphere Concepts, who assumed responsibility for the entire design and creation of the interior.

www.vlassakverhulst.be   www.sphereconcepts.be

The main bathroom is in fitted Jura with painted solid oak. Shower with natural-stone walls and a built-in solarium.

IDYLLIC SURROUNDINGS

This old farmhouse, situated in the green outskirts of Antwerp on a castle estate, has recently been completely restored by AID Architects (G. Van Zundert / K. Bakermans). The house is in idyllic countryside, with a garden of several hectares that merges with the surrounding nature. The restoration was kept as authentic as possible, with no superfluous adornment: the aim was to create a calm living environment for a young, dynamic family, with a focus on functionality and space. This no-nonsense approach has resulted in a simple and honest atmosphere. The use of old, natural materials in combination with some contemporary elements has also helped to create a special, distinctive feel in this home.

www.aidarchitecten.be

DEDICATED TO HARMONY

A haven of tranquillity set at the heart of a 6-hectare park: the countryside at the town's doorstep. Transformed by the architects A.R.P.E (Antoine de Radiguès) and the general construction firm Macors, this small, resolutely New England-style manor house is dedicated to harmony. Lionel Jadot created the interior design and these beautiful bathrooms.

lioneljadot@yahoo.fr   www.macors.be

A SPACIOUS BATHROOM IN A THATCHED BARN

Sphere Concepts were behind the total renovation of this listed farmhouse constructed at the beginning of the last century, and situated on an estate of thirty hectares. The complete interior design, including the materials and colours, was proposed and developed by Sphere in consultation with the owner. The old outbuildings and the house have new functions. The thatched barn now houses the parents' rooms, including the spacious bathroom.

www.sphereconcepts.be

Walls and bathtub in tadelakt.

A BATHROOM SUITE IN A TWO-STOREY LOFT

This loft on two storeys is situated in a former studio with a house behind. The space was completely redesigned by the Olivier Dwek architectural studio in collaboration with architect Mathieu DeWitte. The bathroom *en suite* with the dressing room was designed by Olivier Dwek. The extension of the bathroom taps (next to the freestanding bath) is a Dwek creation and the concrete basins are from this architecture studio. The shower is behind the washbasins.

www.olivierdwek.com

HARMONY OF COLOURS

The rainshower in this bathroom designed by the Schellen architectural
studio is screened off with a large, clear glass wall.
Warm harmony of colours in the dark stained oak veneer of the suspended
vanity unit and the dark-brown glass mosaic of the bath surround.

www.schellen.be

A SEARCH FOR AUTHENTICITY

A few years ago, a couple of decorators and architects, seduced by nature and minimalism, moved into a XIXth century farmhouse. Antiquities and contemporary art converge in an atmosphere that is continuously renewed, at the cadence of their acquisitions. The owners of this place, being used at the same time as single family home and Polyèdre's headquarter, warmly welcome you twice a year. Restructuring spaces, as in this old 1895 fruit plantation, searching for quality materials, authentic furniture, items of curiosity, colours and fabrics and combining them in a contemporary ambience. Such is the challenge assigned to Henri-Charles and Natasha Hermans.

www.polyedre.be

The bathroom has a rounded design bath. The toilet vanity is made in aged oak at the Polyèdre work studio.
The shower corner and toilets are illuminated by a charming bull's eye window.

ENGLISH ROOTS

Within a setting of lovely park trees, Costermans Villa
Projects realised a timeless English manor. The architectural
design and use of materials have strong English roots.

www.costermans-projecten.be

Sand-coloured tones predominate the walk-in wardrobe and bathroom of this suite. Washing stand and bath are covered in a warmer marble, Breccia Pernice. The natural stone floor and walls are made of Crema Marfil, the taps are bronze-coloured and made by the Belgian manufacturer RVB.

The guest bathrooms are designed with an English wink, the natural stone is of Iberian origin. "Dark and Light Emperador", a warm brown veined type of marble.

BATHING IN WHITE

Vincent Bruggen builds beautiful houses with a Canadian wood skeleton construction.
The bathroom in this country house baths in monochrome white: the oak
planks have been lacquered white, the doors and bath surroundings have been
painted white, the washbasin are covered with white Carrara marble...

www.vincentbruggen.be

This bathroom has been designed by the Vincent Bruggen interior team.

A HARMONY OF WOOD AND
BIANCO STATUARIO MARBLE

Interior architect Filip Vanryckeghem (iXtra) designed the plan for
this attic room with an en-suite bathroom and shower.
He came up with a surprising combination of wooden planks
and high-quality Bianco Statuario marble.
The interior work was carried out by Interieur Vandeputte (Proven, Poperinge).
Van den Weghe were responsible for the stonework.

www.ixtra.be   www.vandenweghe.be

SUBTLE NUANCES

This bathroom is situated in a roof apartment opposite the Fondation Cartier in Paris. Olivier Lempereur was asked by a couple of art lovers to create a comfortable, contemporary space.

www.olivierlempereur.com

Subtle nuances created by the different finishes of the bluestone in the bathroom.

The spacious shower in bush-hammered bluestone.

MINIMALIST LUXURY WITH SUBTLE ASIAN TOUCHES

Olivier Lempereur transformed the entire top floor of a Haussmann-style building.
The interior is characterised by minimalist luxury enhanced with subtle Asian touches.
The suspended washbasin is made of grey-beige natural stone, cut from a single
block. Each of the mirrors conceals a storage space and reflects the Paris sky.
In the background are two symmetrical spaces, including the
impressive shower with its small platinum mosaic tiles.

www.olivierlempereur.com

In this shower with its many reflections, the floor is divided into four large natural-stone tiles that stand free of the walls.

The bath in black and platinum mosaic is held within an illuminated basin of grey-beige natural stone.
A small dressing table is completely concealed behind a panel of sandblasted wood.

SHADES OF BEIGE AND GREY

This bathroom, designed by Olivier Lempereur in a Paris apartment, has
been built in a grey natural stone with a smoothed finish on the lower
section and a lightly bush-hammered finish on the upper part.
The shower is clad with natural stone in two shades, with a vertical structure.

www.olivierlempereur.com

A CITY OASIS

This apartment is on the top floor of a building built in 1911 in the heart of Milan. It took Romeo Sozzi, designer and owner of Promemoria, almost two years to complete this project: a gallery for his art, with only the most exclusive pieces on display, and an oasis where he can relax and enjoy the peace and quiet. The predominant colour is an unusual shade, close to hazelnut.

www.promemoria.com

A Gong table in matt nickel in the bathroom. with a
mirror with gold-leaf surround above the bath.

Shower curtain with buttonholes and rings in matt nickel.

↖
Matt-nickel mirror. washing
unit with linen finish and
Rosa lamps.
A leather-covered cabinet
and a bronze towel rail.

LUXURY OF SPACE

The Brussels design company Ensemble & Associés were asked to fit out a 200m² apartment in the heart of Brussels. The key words were: open, calm, pure. Luxury of space, superiority of materials and quality of finish: these three elements are of prime importance to Ensemble & Associés in all of their projects.

www.ensembleetassocies.be

A pure and monochrome white for this bathroom in composite stone.
The washbasin surround has been extended into the shower through the glass screen behind the bath.
The opal-glass screen between the bathroom and the bedroom allows through the perfect amount of light.

ESSENTIALIST PENTHOUSE

The space in this penthouse consisted of a surface area of 300m² with ceilings of between three and five metres high. The location of the structural and technical elements of the apartment had already been fixed. Julie Brion and Tanguy Leclercq took on this penthouse in shell form and were responsible for the finishing. The structural and technical elements were all carefully concealed so as not to spoil the look of the apartment. In consultation with the client, views and flow-through areas were created between the various spaces, ensuring that the whole apartment is bathed in an abundance of natural light.

www.brionleclercq.com

The bathroom has lacquered panels and white marble throughout. The linear appearance of the walls is accentuated by the identical niches in the shower and toilet.
The sober design of the central block harmonises with the expert use of lacquered panels and white marble.

TIMELESS LUXURY

CarterTyberghein were asked to design the interior of the penthouse apartment on the 18th floor of a building situated in the Docklands with dramatic views along the Thames. They were given the dimensions and produced schematic layouts to turn the penthouse into a three-bedroom luxury apartment. The walls of the master bathroom are clad with Statuary Venato marble. The mirror conceals a TV screen and the vanity unit is finished in metal leaf with a Thassos marble top.

www.cartertyberghein.com

Mother-of-pearl mosaic behind the bath contrasts with the Statuary Venato marble.

A combined steam and shower room with a cantilevered Thassos marble bench.

COMFORT, ELEGANCE AND LIGHT

Esther Gutmer completely redesigned the interior of a beautiful country estate.
The house was classic in style and not well-suited to modern needs.
The new design ensures the four member of the family comfort, elegance, light and
functionality throughout the whole house, including the spacious bathrooms.

www.esthergutmer.be

The bath has been partially built into the floor.
The wall behind the bath conceals a toilet and a shower.

↖
Beige marble and polished
pear wood were selected for
the main bathroom.

A FLAVOUR OF NEW ENGLAND

Interior architect Esther Gutmer was commissioned to add a flavour of New England
to a newly built villa in the centre of Knokke-Zoute on the Belgian coast.

www.esthergutmer.be

Small mosaic tiles in smoothed Carrara marble have been used on the floor and in the shower of this master bathroom.

White Carrara marble.

↖
A washing unit in mahogany.

HARMONY IN WHITE AND BROWN

Esther Gutmer completely renovated this duplex apartment in a three-storey building dating from 1921. The distinctive character of this home, with its perfectly symmetrical semi-hexagonal shape, lies in the way all of the rooms open to the front of the building. Esther Gutmer has redivided the internal space, and also redesigned all of the details of the walls, the floors, the ceilings and the woodwork.

www.esthergutmer.be

RESTFUL AND OPEN

This magnificently situated seaside apartment (ca. 110m^2) was designed by Stephanie Laporte as a holiday home for a family with three children and several grandchildren. The task involved making optimal use of the available space. All of the existing interior walls, floors and ceilings were demolished. The use of light colours and simple materials has created a very restful and open environment, in spite of the demanding specifications.

www.stephanielaporte.be

The bathroom and shower have been clad in natural stone.

CONTRASTS OF WOOD AND NATURAL STONE

The owner of an old farmhouse asked interior architect Stephanie Laporte to make a
very simple design that would still respect the historical character of the house.
The master bathroom has a freestanding bath. Stephanie Laporte plays
with contrasts of wood and natural stone in this project.

www.stephanielaporte.be

ECCENTRIC AND ECLECTIC

The client who commissioned Stephanie Laporte for this loft is a flamboyant
French collector of antiques and art: eccentric and eclectic.
An old, dilapidated warehouse in the city centre was opened up by the demolition of
some of the buildings, allowing extra light into the lofts behind (the client lives in a
loft on the ground floor and his teenage daughters live in another loft upstairs).
The loft on the first floor has a painting of a view of New York in the foreground. This
piece has a cloakroom, toilet and a freestanding washing unit in black mosaic.

www.stephanielaporte.be

The bathroom in the ground-floor loft with a combination of dark parquet, custom made furniture in dark-tinted wood and Moroccan zelliges.
The central unit connects the bedroom and bathroom.
The shower is finished in black zelliges throughout.

SOBER AND SERENE

The parents' bathroom in this project by Stephanie Laporte
adjoins the dressing room and bedroom.
The bath and wall are clad with Corian, combined with a beige floor.

www.stephanielaporte.be

INTIMACY IN A VOLUPTUOUS SETTING

The idea behind this open bath / dressing / bed area in a contemporary
loft, was to offer intimacy in a voluptuous setting.
Interior architect Nathalie Van Reeth designed the bathroom
in slate and varnished MDF cupboards.
The open shower with adjacent hammam is clad with small black marble mosaic.

nathalie.vanreeth@skynet.be

MONASTIC ATMOSPHERE

Both bathrooms in this Nathalie Van Reeth project, a picturesque
coast villa, radiate the same sober monastic atmosphere.
All floors, washbasins and bathtubs have a brown sandstone
finish. The walls have been cemented.

nathalie.vanreeth@skynet.be

THE TIMELESS BEAUTY OF CALACATTA MARBLE

A classical residence underwent a thorough metamorphosis, spurred on by Nathalie
Van Reeth. The house was fully stripped, down to the basic structure.
Materials and colour were added subtly to accentuate the serene atmosphere.
Interior architect Nathalie Van Reeth chose a beautiful Calacatta
marble for the floor, the bath surrounds and the shower wall.

nathalie.vanreeth@skynet.be

MEM faucets by Dornbracht and lighting by Cubetto.

A HOLIDAY FEEL

For this home, idyllically situated in Walloon Brabant, the challenge was to reconcile
a wooden building structure with a contemporary interior. A successful project:
when you enter this home, you are overwhelmed by a true holiday feel.
Architect: Gregory Dellicour. Building contractor: Mi Casa.

www.ensembleetassocies.be

The vanity unit in the main bathroom is made of sandblasted oak and composite stone.
Taps by Dornbrecht (model MEM).

TWO BATHROOMS IN A DUPLEX APARTMENT

These bathrooms have been designed by Ensemble & Associés in a 350 m² duplex apartment. The main bathroom floor is finished in anthracite grey, brushed composite stone. The bathtub and the washbasins are covered with Bianco Zeus. Joinery in sandblasted, stained larch and lacquered medium. The vanity unit in the guest bathroom is made of beveka wood. The floor is clad with Cotto d'Este.

www.ensembleetassocies.be

ODETTE EN VILLE

"Chez Odette" is the ideal base for city residents to explore the remote Gaume region. Today there is also "Odette en ville", to re-experience this success story in Brussels as well. A place like no other in the capital, truly worthy of a metropolis. Eight rooms that respect the distinctive whole of this residence to the tiniest detail, with a harmonious mix of original mouldings, natural materials and details from yesteryear. The bathrooms have been designed in the same spirit. Creative Director: Alisa Thiry. General Contractor : 3° Bureau.

www.ensembleetassocies.be

A freestanding bathtub by Devon & Devon.

A BATHROOM IN TUSCAN MARBLE

This bathroom in Tuscan marble from Dominique Desimpel (walls, floor, bath and washbasin surrounds) is a creation by Philip Simoen. MEM taps by Dornbracht in nickel with a matt finish.

www.tegelsdesimpel.be

CRAFTSMANSHIP IN NATURAL STONE

In this report, Van den Weghe (The Stone Company) shows two
bathroom projects where their craftsmanship is evident.

www.vandenweghe.be

All the natural stone works in this bathroom are also by Van den Weghe.

↖
A surprising combination
of bright colours, a wooden
floor and natural stone
works in exclusive, rare
types of natural stone.

CLASSICAL INSPIRATION

Classical inspiration for these bathrooms
in soft colours from Wood Fashion.

www.woodfashion.com

The wood in this bathroom created by Wood Fashion is ever-present.

TRANQUIL AND SERENE

Tranquillity and serenity in this bathroom designed by Kultuz.
The earth colours and shades of brown and grey are
combined with white walls and porcelain washbasins.

www.kultuz.be

HARMONY OF WHITE IN AN ANCIENT CASTLE

It took two years for the efforts of Hendrik Vermoortel and Ingrid Lesage to transform Kasteel Ter Heyde, supposedly founded on a castle-mound structure with origins in the fourteenth century, into a contemporary castle home.

www.buro2.be

The shower cubicles are one of Buro I & II's own designs.

The Corian washstand is a Buro I design. Taps by Grohe. The centrally positioned transparent shower cubicles ensure optimal spaciousness and circulation.

↖
The bell tower has been transformed into a bathroom. The floor and walls have been clad with Bisazza mosaic.
All the thermal installations were created by Develtere.

MODERN PANACHE FOR A CLASSIC VILLA

The owners of a classic villa in the green belt around Brussels
asked the Instore design bureau to design a bathroom and a library for them.
In the end, the whole house was renovated: many traditional decorative
elements, typical of French-style country houses of that period,
were stripped and the house was simplified to its essential volumes and proportions.

www.instore.be

The shower and the wall above the bath are clad with marble mosaic from Moma.

Washstand in white Carrara marble.
Taps by Boffi.

A CLASSIC TOUCH IN A CONTEMPORARY COUNTRY HOUSE

This residence for a family with three growing children was built by architect Bernard De Clerck in a classic eighteenth-century style: he drew his inspiration from a bishop's country seat near Bruges, which dates back to 1750. The quality of the light, the creation of perspectives and the optimal orientation of the rooms were important in the design of this house.

info@bernarddeclerck.be

The floor of the large
bathroom is laid with a
design in old grey Breccia
marble, alternating with
old, soft ochre-coloured
marble. The washbasins are
built into large alcoves. An
interior window above the
bath gives a view through to
the dressing room.

A shower by the large
bathroom.

THE BATHROOMS OF A HISTORIC FINCA

La Carrascosa, a historic finca near Jerez de la Frontera (southern Spain), is situated on the foothills of a wild and untouched scenic area that stretches for around eighty kilometres along the Bay of Cadiz, almost as far as the rock of Gibraltar. The owner, a well-travelled businessman, wanted to create a property that would be easy to use in the warm summer months as well as the sometimes unpredictable winter period. Christine Bekaert transformed the existing buildings, which had previously been closed, into pleasant winter rooms by using warm colours and materials and by integrating many hunting accessories. Michel Ceuterick designed the architectural style of the two new wings, linked by an imposing tower. Thanks to the subtle use of reclaimed materials that were often hundreds of years old, a timeless unity has been created, which flows seamlessly into the existing architecture.

www.christinebekaert.be

The walls of the bathroom were partly clad in zelliges, partly in hand-polished tadellakt. Wall lights and washbasins are in nickel.

Both the shutters and the window can slide open and they overlook a private garden. The floor is laid with pink Gerona marble.

↖
Parts of the bathroom walls
have been clad with hand-
cut zelliges from Fez; the
floor and bath surround
are in marble from Gerona
(Spain). The ceiling is
inspired by a typical
Hispano-Arabic steam bath,
many of which can still be
found in South Andalusia.

FRENCH MASSANGIS

A historic country house, built with a perfect sense of proportion and balance, has been renovated by architect Jean-Paul Decordier. Marc Stellamans, in close consultation with the owners, was responsible for all the interior furnishings. The resolutely modern design and the restrained styling create a fascinating contrast with the classic proportions of the country house. The bathroom is completely clad in French Massangis limestone.

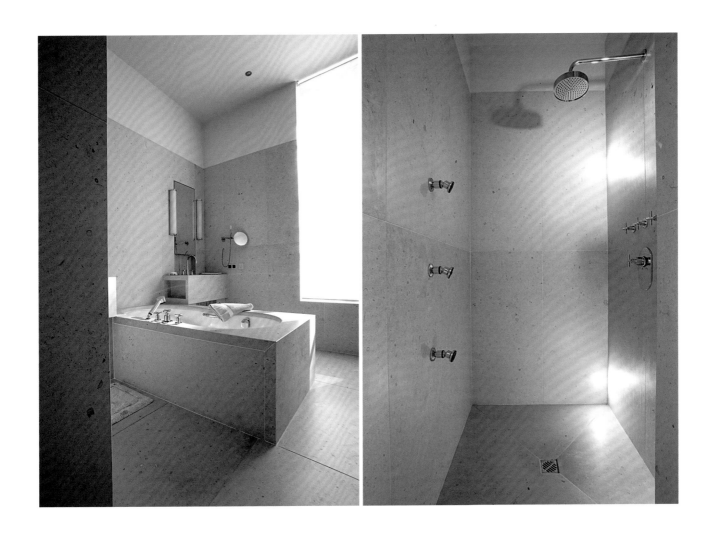

INSPIRED BY THE CLASSIC POLDER FARMHOUSE

Architect Stéphane Boens designed these bathrooms in a country house inspired by the classic Flemish polder farmhouse.

www.stephaneboens.be

A monastic atmosphere in the bath- and shower-rooms, clad with old marble from Carrara.

IN BALANCE

This farmhouse was created by Stéphane Boens.
The owners also use the house as a showroom for am projects, their interior-design company.
Their work is more a philosophy of life than simple decoration. They create
timeless environments and living spaces that are perfectly in balance with
the lifestyle of their clients. They decorated this house themselves.

www.stephaneboens.be   www.amprojects.be

The bathroom floor has been laid with reclaimed Italian Carrara marble that was found in Spain. The steam cabinet has been finished in tadelakt. The taps and bathroom accessories are distributed by am projects.

Both of the doors in the wall behind the bath can be opened to create an atmosphere of space. With the doors closed, these rooms appear to be completely separate. The bath (Wall Strip by Aquamass) is the eye-catching feature in this design: its lines (almost the shape of a curling leaf) merge seamlessly with the white wall behind.

OPTIMAL INTEGRATION

A London art collector asked Mark Mertens (am projects) to refurbish her residence and provide for the interior decoration. The aim was to design a timeless, minimalist interior. The decision was taken to maintain the existing original elements of the residence, and restore these where necessary. All fitted cupboards and bathrooms were designed by Mark Mertens to enable optimal integration into the existing architecture. A limited range of materials was used for both bathrooms: Italian Carrara marble and Belgian bluestone.

www.amprojects.be

CHARM, PEACE AND QUIET

This renovation project was entrusted to Sphere Concepts. They contacted architect Gerd Van Zundert (AID Architects) to adapt the outer walls and to bring these into the correct proportions, after Sphere Concepts had designed the interior layout. The previous layout of the villa was dated, and Sphere Concepts replaced this with an interior that radiates charm, and in particular peace and quiet. Axes and throughviews were incorporated where possible, the right materials were chosen, and all colours and finishing trims were decided on with a view to achieving a harmonious and balanced end result. The renovation work was meticulously carried out by the PDK building firm in Deurne.

www.sphereconcepts.be

The bathroom is entirely fitted out with Boffi, even for the made-to-measure items at the end of the bath and the washbasins.

COSY MINIMALISM

Interior designer Dries Dols was faced with a major challenge when he took on this project. He had to create a timeless contemporary interior in a conventional residence with a lot of traditional elements. And what's more, all the members of the family had their own very specific (and differing) views on what makes a successful living environment. For Dries Dols it was an enthralling assignment, and one in which he has succeeded wonderfully well. Basing himself on the traditional elements, the designer chose materials with taut lines. The end result looks particularly restful, minimalist and yet cosy.

www.dols.nl   www.elfcreators.com

Two washbasins (for him and for her) were entirely sheathed in solid waterproof finish-lacquered oak.
This bathroom connects to the dressing room.

↖
The bath was fitted in a
raised dais like an island
beneath the window, so that
the sun coming through
the window can be enjoyed
in the evening. The dais
also has a towel rack. A
dispensing cupboard has
been incorporated alongside
the bath, to house all
bathroom bits and pieces.

A SERENE ATMOSPHERE

The owners discovered this farmhouse on an overcast day in May. It was not an obvious choice as somewhere to go and live, but they dreamed of life in the country and saw nothing but prospects in the farmhouse's dilapidated state. When the restoration was carried out, the conscious decision was taken to go for a contemporary approach, involving all the materials being cleaned up and all mod cons being incorporated. Integrating the surrounding landscape into the residence as much as possible was one of the explicit tasks facing architect Gerd Van Zundert, who has succeeded extremely well in doing just that.

www.moka-projects.com   www.moka-vanille.com

The client wanted a serene atmosphere in the bathroom. All wet walls were finished in tadelakt, and adjoining these, the colour range was continued in distemper.

The built-in toilet is a light-hearted nod to the sanitary fittings of the old days that had been found here and there in the dilapidated property. On the rough-wood oak floorboards – here around a tadelakt formwork bath – the water rings are still visible in some places for a natural effect.

UNDERSTATED ELEGANCE

A rather dull French-style house from the 1960s was transformed to create a spacious,
up- to-date home that fulfils all of the client's requirements for comfort.
Light and space were key elements of this design by 'Aksent.

www.aksent-gent.be

A spacious shower in white stone with a rain shower head.

↖
The bathroom has a sober
finish in white stone and
smoked oak. The wall
behind the bath is in brown
marble mosaic.

WELLNESS IN A FRENCH ALPS CHALET

This mountain chalet is set amidst picturesque scenery in the French Alps. The traditional architecture was reinterpreted so that the magnificent views could be enjoyed to best effect, whilst the interior is a luxurious mixture of style, comfort and a modern lifestyle. The design team of Moulder, Laxer + Salter of F3 Architects in London worked together with Base Contracts and local professionals in order to complete this extraordinary residence and have it ready for immediate occupation. Base Contracts specialises in exclusive residential construction throughout the world. F3 Architects is a design office for architecture and interior fittings, which offers totally integrated design services. This dynamic team creates inspiring living environments with a harmonious transition from interior architecture to decorative furnishing.

www.f3architects.co.uk   www.basecontracts.com

The bespoke designed spa by F3 utilizes the latest technologies and combines natural stone, wood and bronze detailing by London specialists Based Upon. The spa includes a massage room, sauna, steam hammam with ice cave, pool and shower.

↖
Steam hammam
with ice cave.

OLD WOOD, TINTED CONCRETE AND GLASS MOSAIC

This project by Marina Wenger (Version M) shows a subtle mix of contemporary and traditional chalet style, with timeless materials and objects.

www.versionm.com

The hammam is covered in Sicis glass mosaic.

A carefully measured mix of old wood and tinted concrete for this bathroom.

↖
The washbasin in enamelled, bronze-coloured ceramics. Accessories in leather and brushed stainless steel.

A BATHROOM IN CRANS-MONTANA

This elegant apartment, located in a building of recent construction
in the centre of Crans-Montana, was designed and built entirely by
interior architect Marina Wenger and her Version M team.
It boasts a beautiful mountain view.

www.versionm.com

↖
The Indian panels separate
the bedroom from the
bathroom. Washbasins in
chocolate-coloured Corian.

CONTEMPORARY APPROACH

In this project by Frank Missotten Villabouw, an authentic architectural style was combined with a contemporary interior. The chalet is of recent construction.

www.missotten.be

An out-and-out contemporary approach for the bathrooms, with wenge tinted cupboards and sanitary fittings by Starck.

A LOFT WITH A BREATHTAKING VIEW OF THE CAPITAL

This loft, situated on the top floor of a converted industrial building, has
been completely reorganised by interior architect Anne Derasse.
All of the functions flow together in the same space. The master bedroom with
bathroom and dressing room is alongside this large central rectangle.
The entire space and the fitted furniture were designed by Anne Derasse.

www.annederasse.be

The main bathroom with a wash unit in lavastone. Lighting with additional LEDs for decoration. In the background, a dressing room in polished oak beside the master bedroom.

The large shower beneath a light well. Dornbracht taps. To the left of the shower, a bench with storage space beneath.

↖
The en-suite bathroom with the bedroom and dressing room: shades of grey-blue and grey-green in harmony with lavastone.

A LUMINOUS MINIMALISM

Olivier Michel, the founder and driving force behind Upptown, is one of the most talked-about project developers of recent years. In a very desirable area of Uccle (Brussels region), he discovered a group of dilapidated warehouses and garages, which he soon transformed into a residential project with four ultramodern lofts. The intention was to sell all four properties, but Michel and his wife were so enthusiastic about this project that they joined together two of the lofts for themselves to create one large property of over 600m², with its own garden, a swimming pool and two patio areas. The construction work was entrusted to architect Bruno Corbisier. The Upptown team designed the entire interior: one of the major assets of this visionary property group is the total approach, from supervising the construction of a project to handing over the keys to the satisfied new owners.

The black/white contrast is taken to its extreme in the main bathroom. Custom-made furniture in white Corian with a black glass washbasin. The walls are in black lacquered glass.

The bathtub is by
Aquamass.

EIGHTEENTH-CENTURY INSPIRATION
FOR A COUNTRY MANOR

Architect Bernard De Clerck designed a country manor in a traditional style for a young family that enjoys an informal way of life and being in close contact with nature: quiet, calming and sophisticated. The eighteenth century was an important source of inspiration for this project. Bernard De Clerck created the whole house: outside as well as inside. His clients gave him a great deal of support with this, as did the capable specialists who carried out his designs to the smallest detail. For some rooms (the bathrooms and the bedrooms for the children and guests), he called upon the expertise of interior designer Christine Bekaert.

info@bernarddeclerck.be   www.christinebekaert.be

The daughter's bathroom is fitted with a freestanding bath and an oak washbasin unit.

↖
The master bathroom is in
pale grey and beige tones.
The subtle illumination
is regulated by interior
shutters. The floor is
chequered with old Carrara
and Saint-Anne marble.

THE BATHROOM IN A 1862 LONDON RESIDENCE

This master bathroom in a stately residence in London's Holland Park built in 1862 was designed by Winny Vangroenweghe, architect with Obumex. She created and coordinated the complete renovation and layout of the premises into a timeless and harmonious whole, where the hectic character of the metropolis is quickly forgotten...

www.obumex.be

The master bathroom was created in lava rock by natural stone company Van Den Weghe. Bathroom fittings by Vola.

GREY LAVA ROCK AND GREY SMOKED GLASS

This master bathroom is designed completely from drawings by architect Pascal van der Kelen and finished with grey lava rock and grey smoked glass for the sliding doors.

www.pascalvanderkelen.com

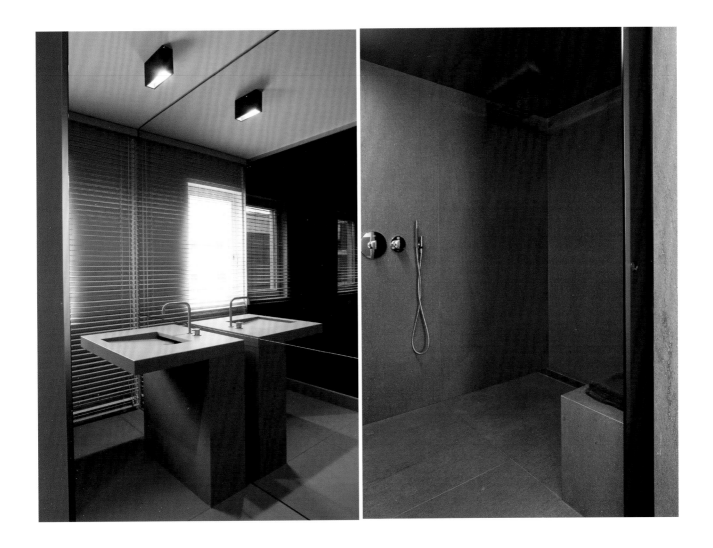

The continuous mirror that reaches the ceiling effectively doubles the space.

CARTE BLANCHE

Interior architect Sarah Lavoine was given a carte blanche for this complete project in the heart of Paris: the transformation of a duplex apartment with 250 m² + 200 m² terraces. The renovation works took a long time because the original kitchen and entrance hall were situated on the upper floor. Sarah Lavoine designed these rooms below, so the eighth floor could be devoted completely to the master bedroom with desk, dressing room, bathroom and wet room. The whole thing was completely redesigned by Sarah Lavoine's team: creation of the spaces, customisation, the succession of volumes...

www.sarahlavoine.com

The wet room is completely covered with black mosaic.
Bathroom fittings by Tara van Dornbracht.

↖
A sober, monochrome whole
in taupe-coloured Azul
Valverde stone for this main
bathroom. The washbasins
are carved stone.
In the background is a large
glass wall with mirror effect
that hides the wet room.

A RIGID TOTAL DESIGN

The design of this low energy home, created by the architect Annik Dierckx, is timeless and practical. The newest materials and most recent technologies were used. The bathrooms are situated in such a way that they are accessible both from the corridor and directly from the bedrooms. The proportions in the rooms, the colour palette and the choice of materials tantalize the senses of every visitor, who immediately feels at home. The rigid total design by the hand of a single architect, who designed both the interior and exterior of the home, exudes warmth and harmony.

www.adarchitectuur.be

TIMELESS, OPEN AND SPACIOUS

Interior architect Dennis T'Jampens transformed an old factory space of 200 m² to a timeless, open and spacious loft. The home exudes restraint and unity: straight lines, symmetrical structure, a combination of warm, lavish materials like oak and weathered marble and the white lacquered joinery ensure balance and calm. Bathroom, dressing room and bedroom are three separate rooms but give the impression of being one whole. There is a repetition of the materials used here as well. The freestanding bath (made in Corian) and the rough marble mosaic wall (Hullebusch) are real "eye catchers" in this distinctive loft.

www.dtj-interiorarchitect.be

THE BATHROOM OF A SPACIOUS PENTHOUSE

This wonderfully located penthouse was designed by Filip Glorieux
and his team as the main residence for an active family.
The task consisted of connecting three apartments into a single residential
whole with different functions that fulfil the wishes of the occupants.
Filip Glorieux and his team realised the design, execution
and coordination of this unique total project.

www.filipglorieux.be

OPTIMISING THE SPACE

The floor plan of this magnificently situated apartment by the coast was adapted by Minus at the client's request to optimise the space within the limited area. The built in furnishings were made in grades of white, strengthened with a number of sand coloured highlights that immediately elicit a holiday feel.

www.minus.be

A SEAMLESS FLOW

The client's request for the project, designed by the architect Tom Vanbiervliet:
reflecting sober and timeless architecture from outside to inside.
The first floor is conceived as a single large space; around a central axis the
dressing room, office, bedroom and bathroom were situated. All the rooms can be
closed with sliding doors but if open these seamlessly flow into each other.
The same material was used everywhere for both floors and walls. The warmth of natural
materials like wood and rough Carrara marble perfectly suit the rigid smooth walls.

www.minus.be

A WARM TOUCH

As one of the few modern homes in the surrounding, the atmosphere of the contemporary architecture continues indoors: large and high rooms with a lot of light, and the use of sober materials in a tight framework.
Obumex's design still results in an interior with a warm touch, the natural materials, the shades of grey outside and white inside, the balanced colour packages, with here and there a contemporary accent.
This is a project that is fully designed, implemented and co-ordinated by Obumex.

www.obumex.be

The dressing with dark wooden cabinets with solid brass handles and a drawer console covered with leather.

↖
The dark wood and bronze
details were also used here.
A custom-made carpet
around the bath.

SOBER AND MASCULINE

Interior Architects Brigitte Boiron and John-Paul Welton continue their cooperation further and provide the complete renovation of this apartment of 320 m² located in a historic building in Geneva. They created a timeless and luxurious universe. The company Project Design was responsible for the complete renewal of the rooms.

www.projectdesign.ch   www.weltondesign.com

The woodwork of this bathroom is by Obersson. A sink in black marble, sink and shower by Dornbracht (Citterio design). A polished concrete floor and wall.

↖

This bathroom is covered with Béton Grey 900x450 (Mirage collection) by Workshop. Photography by Alexis Reynaud. Aquamass bathtub, sink by Toscoquattro and floor mixer tap by Axor (Hansgrohe).

TRANSPARENCY, LIGHTNESS AND LUMINOSITY

Located on top of a promontory, this villa was completely restructured "feet in the water" style, and enlarged by GEF Réalisations, the office for interior design. Transparency, lightness and luminosity were the keywords in this project.

gef@wanadoo.fr

187

THE BATHROOM OF A LOFT IN AMSTERDAM

Despite the fact that this house was handed over completely new,
the basic structure still had to be adapted completely.
Rob Zeelen of Zeth Interior architecture & implementation, together with Lucien van
de Ven of B-Dutch and Jos van Zijl (Jos van Zijl Design) designed the space.
The client wanted a sober, functional and timeless interior,
in which the designers succeeded admirably.

www.zeth.nl   www.josvanzijl.nl

The bathroom was designed by Jos van Zijl. A bath by Agape, taps by Vola and lighting by Maretti.
Specially made cupboard wall designed by Jos van Zijl and produced by B-Dutch.
The shower is of the make Byos (Jos van Zijl design).

SOLID OAK AND TADELAKT

Am projects, Mark Mertens got the commission to design and complete the interior of this farmhouse in West Flanders. Am projects were also in the running for the interior décor. The aim was a timeless, minimalist interior, which still radiated a certain warmth. Much use was made of natural materials throughout this project. Colour accents were added by the furniture and paintwork.

www.amprojects.be

The bath surround was made by Am projects in solid oak.

↖
Bathroom in tadelakt
and oak.

RUSTIC INSPIRATION

This countryside villa was designed by the Demyttenaere architectural studio from Knokke. Sand's Company, the interior-design firm that works closely with Demyttenaere, took care of the complete interior of this idyllically situated house.

www.myth.be   www.sandscompany.be

In the bathroom Azul Fatima natural stone has been combined with doors in solid brushed and oiled oak. The shower has been clad with antique Megaron Lapideum marble mosaic of 5x5 cm (Botticino on net).

METAMORPHOSIS OF AN OLD COACH HOUSE

This coach house, dating from the end of the nineteenth century and situated in south Antwerp, has been restored in an authentic way by interior architect Ariane von Rothkirch and adapted to modern requirements for comfort. She used natural materials (such as wood, stone, marble and lime paints) with the intention of creating a contemporary home in an historic setting.

decorvan@skynet.be

The main bathroom, finished in Arabescato marble, which has been installed in an open-book pattern in the shower. Taps by Volevatch.

Two old food troughs have been transformed into washbasins. Above are mirrors with driftwood frames. Wooden floor in smoked oak. The shower is clad with bluestone.

PERFECTION IN CUSTOM-FITTED NATURAL STONE

This is a creation by Villabouw Sels and their interior architect Steven Van Dooren.
All of the work in natural stone has been carried out by Van den Weghe.

www.vandenweghe.be

Bushhammered (anti-slip) Spanish Cenia marble has been combined with Greek Golden Chios in the master bathroom.

THE RENOVATION OF AN EXCLUSIVE DREAM HOME

Following a successful career in business, Alexander Cambron now creates around three completely ready-to-use, top-quality residential projects a year, in both contemporary and timelessly classic designs. These are "pret-à-habiter" homes for top executives and their families, with the focus entirely on the wishes and requirements of the new owners. The homes provide the ideal setting for the hobbies of the lady and gentleman of the house, a paradise for the children, ample space for sport and relaxation, a fully wired home office, a collection of cars and a workshop, a wine cellar, home-automation systems, music and security and a beautiful fully grown garden with space for a horse and pets.

www.alexandershouses.com   www.fabathome.be

The colour-coordinated bathroom in beige natural stone with illuminated white onyx walls beside the bath and in the shower.

↖
An overflow bath with
a ceiling-mounted tap.
The sliding doors are
in leather, in the same
colour as the stone.

PERFECTION DOWN TO THE FINEST DETAILS

A privately owned small castle, built in 1879, was meticulously renovated by interior designer Sigisbert Engelbosch (Metiendo Vivendum). It was a difficult commission for Den Stal, the company that renewed and perfectly renovated all the woodwork here, everything completely made-to-measure. The right choice of wood sort and the fittings by Dauby gave each room a different aura: sometimes more classical, with the mouldings and the adapted door, window and furniture fittings, sometimes more playful, but always a demonstration of impeccable taste.

www.dauby.be   www.metiendovivendum.com   www.denstal.be

The fish bone parquet was also fully renovated and renewed where necessary. The playful furniture tops stand out perfectly here, as though it has always been this way.

The solid cupboard is fully made-to-measure with matching marble tablet and furniture top by Giara in natural bronze.

ART AND DESIGN IN A MINIMALIST SETTING

This minimalist house was designed by Alain Demarquette, an architect from northern France, who was commissioned by clients with a passion for contemporary art and design. Senior interior architect Kurt Neirynck from Obumex designed and supervised the home interior. One of the most important sources of inspiration for this house was the Fondation Beyeler in Basel, a Renzo Piano creation. Grey, white and black are the basic colours that recur throughout this project: this virtually monochrome palette ensures a streamlined and simple look throughout.

www.obumex.be   www.ademarquette-architecte.com

A WEALTH OF LIGHT

A skylight in this bathroom designed by In Tempo by Luc Leroi allows in a wealth of light, yet provides the necessary privacy. Dark-tinted limewood is alternated with bronze and very pale Nozay natural stone. The aim was to create a fresh and airy space that promotes rest and relaxation. Bronze mirror by Promemoria.

www.aksent-gent.be

Pale pebbles have been used for the floor in the children's bathroom.
The insides of the cupboards are sky blue to create a holiday
atmosphere. Three children: three sinks. with adjustable mirrors that
can grow with the children.

A COMBINATION OF ROUGHNESS AND ELEGANCE

The interior architects from 'Aksent created this spacious apartment on the Belgian coast, with its wonderful sea views, selecting the materials and colours in collaboration with Matthijs & Co, general contractors. The warm and subdued atmosphere ensures that the apartment is more than just a holiday home. This is a place that the owners can enjoy all year round.

www.aksent-gent.be

The children's bathrooms were also given a fresh and young look, involving a creative use of materials (rough marble mosaic and strips of slate on the floors and walls, roughened Douglas pine and hand-painted sections for the furniture). Custom-made bronze handles designed by 'Aksent.

↖
The parents' bathroom is in a rough "spazzolato" lime technique. Custom-made furniture and natural stone. Leather towel hooks by Promemoria.

A LARGE AND SPACIOUS DUPLEX PENTHOUSE

This duplex penthouse on the Belgian coast is unusual in many respects. This is a very large apartment with both the charm and floor space (over 1000m^2) of a country house, but with a unique sea view. The home has been finished to a very high standard throughout. Obumex designed and created the ground floor, while interior architect Philip Simoen was responsible for the design of the upstairs rooms, which were then created by Obumex.

www.simoeninterieur.be   www.obumex.be

One of the many bathrooms, here with a walk-in shower. Designed and built by Obumex.

This guestroom and adjoining bathroom were also designed by Philip Simoen.
The walls in the bathroom are in Pietra Piasentina stone.
Tara taps and fittings by Dornbracht.

A guest bathroom in black and silver Bisazza mosaic. Furniture by D-Interieur. Tara taps and fittings by Dornbracht. Design: Philip Simoen.

A TIMELESS ATMOSPHERE IN A CONTEMPORARY APARTMENT BLOCK

Costermans Villaprojects created two floors in this contemporary apartment block: two different styles that are similar in terms of atmosphere and use of colours, with the same restful and understated ambience.

www.costermans-projecten.be

Carrara marble was used in this bathroom as a mosaic on the floor and shower walls.
The marble mosaic makes the shower look warm and inviting.

↖
This modern bathroom has
bronzed walls, with pale
stone surfaces in an even
tone.
The central feature is a cosy
bench.

INNOVATION AS A LEITMOTIF

Hullebusch is a leading family firm specialising in the production and sale of exclusive stone. The company's own production facilities allow them to create unique, personalised finishes and treatments. They produce striking results that surprise and delight private clients, architects and interior designers. Hullebusch's speciality is Belgian bluestone, a timeless and everlasting classic. This is pure, customised work at its most beautiful: Romano style, Cottage, Soignies style, and many other familiar finishes. This finish is also applied to all of the company's marble, which creates a soft and luxurious look. This is perfect timing, as veined marbles are now enjoying a resurgence.

www.hullebusch.com

HAUTE COUTURE IN NATURAL STONE

For thirty years, renowned architects, interior specialists, construction companies and kitchen designers have treated Van den Weghe nv – The Stonecompany as their point of reference for exclusive natural stone. Director Philippe Van den Weghe and his team combine a fine sense for the latest trends in architecture and interiors with great skill and passion for their profession.

www.vandenweghe.be

In this project by designer Nik Mogensen, tumbled mosaic tiles in Marron Emperador are combined with custom-built furniture in Buxy greige.

A RECENTLY BUILT COUNTRY HOUSE
WITH AN AGE-OLD PATINA

Although the country house in this report was constructed only recently, it seems to have a patina of great age. This is not only the result of the consistent use of weathered and reclaimed materials on the exterior, the interior also has a timeless, historic atmosphere. Dankers Decor, who have a royal warrant and are one of the most renowned Belgian decorating companies, created a harmony of colours throughout the whole house, using Arte Constructo's lime paints, coloured with natural pigments: an "à la carte" solution for this beautiful house.

www.hullebusch.com

BATHING IN LIGHT

This bathroom set, created by the interior architect Filip Vanryckeghem (iXtra) forms a part of a renovation project in a bungalow designed by the architect A. Deheyter. The elementary functions of the space (hand basin, bath, shower, sauna) were filled well but simultaneously an extra dimension was also striven for: a project that exudes "wellness". The skylight above the 140x200 cm large bath from Kos provides extra atmosphere both during the day and in the evening. The texture of the coarse walls in natural stone creates additional play with light and shade. In addition to the zenithal light there is also positive lateral daylight, consciously obtained by opening the closed side facade over the entire width and height of the bathroom. Contact with nature outside gives a special dimension.

www.ixtra.be

LIGHT DEFINES THE ATMOSPHERE

Anversa Residential Housing is specialized in the design and total coordination of renovation, restoration and new construction projects: special realizations for special people. This report shows their recently finished project "R25" in Brasschaat. Anversa designed both the architecture and the interior of this home. The light study was provided by Kurve.

www.anversa.be   www.kurve.be

On the first storey all the floors were whitewashed, a finish by Dankers.

SOUL AND FEELING

This rehabilitation takes place in a recently built house of 550 m². The new owner did not identify with the existing spaces and wanted to have a living space that fitted better with their image, so appealed to interior architect Guillaume Da Silva to give "soul and feeling" again to this too conventional architecture.

www.guillaumedasilva.com   www.odiloncreations.be

In the bathroom, the bath tub leaning against American walnut panelling creates the separation to the dressing room. The cladding of the bath is realised in Vinalmont stone.
The monumental shower was realised in tadelakt by Odilon Créations, with a Vinalmont stone floor.

A PANORAMIC VIEW ON THE 12TH FLOOR

This apartment is on the twelfth floor of a new block of flats designed by the Swiss firm of architects Diener und Diener. The family bought the entire floor (three standard apartments), giving them a 360° view of the entire town. The basic design was put together in close cooperation with architect Pascal van der Kelen.

www.pascalvanderkelen.com

The available surface is doubled by the large mirror surfaces.

↖
The master bath and shower room is made of natural stone, synthetic resin, smoked glass and Spanish oak. White-painted wooden blinds filter the cool northern light.

A SPLIT-LEVEL APARTMENT AND A BED & BREAKFAST

The team of interior architects Julie Brion and Tanguy Leclercq has completely renovated a typical Brussels house located in the throbbing heart of the Belgian capital. Their makeover includes a split-level apartment and the resolutely contemporary Urban Rooms, which is a bright and airy bed & breakfast.

www.brionleclercq.com

TIMELESS ELEGANCE

Costermans Villa Projects coordinates construction and interiors for top-quality country houses and residences, particularly in the leafy outskirts of Antwerp. Bathrooms are always a most important aspect of their interiors : they always exude timeless elegance.

www.costermans-projecten.be

Double shower in Branco de Mos slabs and chrome-plated RVB taps.

↖
The master bathroom with
made-to-measure floor
and surface in Branco de
Mos; units in French oak
veneer and lacquered MDF.
Chrome-plated taps by
Dornbracht.

PUBLISHER
BETA-PLUS publishing
www.betaplus.com

PHOTOGRAPHY
Jo Pauwels

DESIGN
Polydem – Nathalie Binart

ISBN 13: 978-90-8944-117-1

© 2012, BETA-PLUS
All rights reserved. No part of this publication may be
reproduced, stored in a retrieval system, or transmitted in any
form or by any means without approval by the publisher.

Coordination production printing and binding :
www.belvedere.nl - André Kloppenberg
Printing and binding: Printer Trento, Italy